50 Quick Ways to

Outstanding Teaching

By Mike Gershon

About the Author

Mike Gershon is a teacher, trainer and writer. He is the author of twenty books on teaching, learning and education, including a number of bestsellers, as well as the co-author of one other. Mike's online resources have been viewed and downloaded more than 2.5 million times by teachers in over 180 countries and territories. He is a regular contributor to the Times Educational Supplement and has created a series of electronic CPD guides for TES PRO. Find out more, get in touch and download free resources at www.mikegershon.com

Training and Consultancy

Mike is an expert trainer whose sessions have received acclaim from teachers across England. Recent bookings include:

- *Improving Literacy Levels in Every Classroom*, St Leonard's Academy, Sussex

- *Growth Mindsets, Effective Marking and Feedback* Ash Manor School, Aldershot

- *Effective Differentiation,* Tri-Borough Alternative Provision (TBAP), London

Mike also works as a consultant, advising on teaching and learning and creating bespoke materials for schools. Recent work includes:

- *Developing and Facilitating Independent Learning,* Chipping Norton School, Oxfordshire

- *Differentiation In-Service Training,* Charles Darwin School, Kent

If you would like speak to Mike about the services he can offer your school, please get in touch by email: mike@mikegershon.com

Other Works from the Same Authors

Available to buy now on Amazon:

How to use Differentiation in the Classroom: The Complete Guide

How to use Assessment for Learning in the Classroom: The Complete Guide

How to use Questioning in the Classroom: The Complete Guide

How to use Discussion in the Classroom: The Complete Guide

How to Teach EAL Students in the Classroom: The Complete Guide

More Secondary Starters and Plenaries

Secondary Starters and Plenaries: History

Teach Now! History: Becoming a Great History Teacher

The Growth Mindset Pocketbook (with Professor Barry Hymer)

How to be Outstanding in the Classroom

Also available to buy now on Amazon, the entire 'Quick 50' Series:

50 Quick and Brilliant Teaching Ideas

50 Quick and Brilliant Teaching Techniques

50 Quick and Easy Lesson Activities

50 Quick Ways to Help Your Students Secure A and B Grades at GCSE

50 Quick Ways to Help Your Students Think, Learn, and Use Their Brains Brilliantly

50 Quick Ways to Motivate and Engage Your Students

50 Quick Ways to Outstanding Teaching

50 Quick Ways to Perfect Behaviour Management

50 Quick and Brilliant Teaching Games

50 Quick and Easy Ways to Outstanding Group Work

50 Quick and Easy Ways to Prepare for Ofsted

50 Quick and Easy Ways Leaders can Prepare for Ofsted

About the Series

The 'Quick 50' series was born out of a desire to provide teachers with practical, tried and tested ideas, activities, strategies and techniques which would help them to teach brilliant lessons, raise achievement and engage and inspire their students.

Every title in the series distils great teaching wisdom into fifty bite-sized chunks. These are easy to digest and easy to apply – perfect for the busy teacher who wants to develop their practice and support their students.

Acknowledgements

As ever I must thank all the fantastic colleagues and students I have worked with over the years, first while training at the Institute of Education, Central Foundation Girls' School and Nower Hill High School and subsequently while working at Pimlico Academy and King Edward VI School in Bury St Edmunds.

Thanks also to Alison and Andrew Metcalfe for a great place to write and finally to Gordon at KallKwik for help with the covers.

Table of Contents

Make failure great!

And Try to Use Misconceptions

Use Great Activities

Inject Some Fun

Run a Tight Ship

Mix It Up

Give Great Feedback

Set Clear Targets

Give Time to Targets

Do Not Fear Repetition

Do Not Fear Silence

Do Not Fear Noise

Set Your Boundaries and Then Police Them

Take Risks

Try Things Out

Reflect

Survey Your Students

Start With Success

End With Humour

Get Organised

Train Your Students

Facilitate

Think Carefully Before Giving Out Grades

Make It Personal

Ask Exciting Questions

Play to Your Strengths

Consider Your Weaknesses

Be the Leader

Challenge Yourself

Think Literacy

A Brief Request

Introduction

Welcome to '50 Quick Ways to Outstanding Teaching.'

Outstanding teaching means teaching which helps students make brilliant progress. It means teaching which facilitates great learning. And it means teaching which meets the needs of every pupil, which inspires them, engages them and helps them to fulfil their potential.

Every entry in this books aims to show you how to make your teaching outstanding.

Every entry gives you an idea, strategy, activity or technique which is practical, straightforward and effective.

Every entry will help you to teach brilliant lessons over and over again.

So read on and enjoy! I hope the entries which follow give you everything you need to be outstanding, both for yourself and for your students.

Plan, Plan, Plan

01 Planning is the backbone of outstanding teaching. If you plan well, and by that I mean with the needs of your students in mind, you will be much more likely to teach outstanding lessons.

Preparation is a means by which to avoid failure when the heat is on. Good preparation underpins success. This is as true in teaching as in any other walk of life. Planning helps you to ensure the experience pupils have during your lessons is the best one possible.

It is a good idea to prepare lessons well in advance of their delivery date. This will allow you to make tweaks and adaptations based on the information you elicit from your classes. For example, it might be that you need to spend a little longer on a certain topic than you expected. By planning well ahead you can respond more flexibly to such situations than would otherwise be the case.

But Not Too Much

02 Having just extolled the virtues of planning let me add a caveat. Don't plan too much.

All virtues can slip over into vice if we pay them too much heed. Consider the brave woman who becomes reckless or the prudent man who becomes a miser.

Over-planning stymies flexibility. It can also lead to lessons which are about the planning itself, rather than the learning students are supposed to be doing.

In essence, planning is all about providing yourself with a clear framework which you can use to ensure your pupils make good progress. As such, it should contain enough material to promote great learning but not so much that you are devoting a disproportionate amount of time to it.

Remain Flexible

03 In the last two entries I have mentioned the importance of flexibility.

Teaching is ultimately an exercise in communication; it concerns the communication which takes place between you and your students.

Take a step back for a moment and imagine being involved in a conversation in which the other person delivers a series of pre-prepared lines which do not respond to, let alone acknowledge, anything you have said. Clearly this would not be a great conversation (and would it even be a conversation *at all?*).

In the classroom, flexibility lets us respond to our students – to their mood, their understanding, the speed at which they are working and so on.

Flexible, agile teaching will always be closer to outstanding. This is because it more closely matches the learning and the activities to the needs of the students.

Listen to your Gut

04 Sometimes, you need to put aside all the advice, theories and research and listen to your gut. Not always. Because, if we only listened to our guts, then it is likely we would make many mistakes or miss many benefits.

But sometimes your gut needs to come into play.

For example, you might be teaching a lesson with which neither you nor your students can engage, despite repeated attempts. Your brain might tell you to keep on going...but your gut would say otherwise.

It would tell you to change things, to forget about what you had planned and to do something else entirely. In this case, it would be right.

So, get used to listening to your gut and, when it feels like it's telling you the right thing, go with it.

Listen to your Students

05 Because your students have a lot of information about your lessons. More, perhaps, than you are able to access on your own.

Listening to your students can give you an insight into what is going well and what might need to be changed. This, in turn, will lead to better lessons (and outstanding teaching). Here are five ways you can listen to your pupils:

- Hand out questionnaires for them to fill in.

- Lead a discussion focussing on the teaching and learning which happens in your class.

- Observe how your pupils interact with and respond to the lessons you create.

- See whether the work students produce in your lessons is in line with what you are expecting.

- Create an end-of-unit review sheet for pupils to complete.

Elicit Information Wherever You Can

06 Information is vital in the classroom. The more information you elicit, the more accurately you will understand where your students are at and what you need to do to ensure your teaching meets their needs.

You can elicit information in many different ways. These include:

- Through observation

- Through asking questions

- Through listening

- Through marking work

- Through review activities

You can also elicit information through whole-class feedback techniques. For a range of these, see my free resource available at www.mikegershon.com.

Use the Information You Elicit

07 Having elicited information about your students' learning, use it to adapt your teaching. Doing so is an important part of outstanding teaching. Here's why:

Eliciting information places you in a stronger position than the converse. It gives you a better understanding of where students are at and where they need to go next. Using this information sees you adapting your lessons, the feedback you give and the way in which you communicate.

These adaptations will bring your teaching more closely into line with the needs of your students. Therefore, your pupils will likely make much better progress than would otherwise be the case.

The message is clear.

Elicit information about pupils' learning and then use this information to adapt your teaching.

Check Progress

08 Checking progress means seeing, during the course of the lesson, where your students are at in terms of their learning.

You can check the progress of individual students, of groups, or of the whole class.

Ways to check progress include:

- Asking questions

- Observation

- Listening

- Reading pupils' work

- Review activities

- Discussions

- Whole-class feedback techniques (see entry six)

Regularly checking progress means you can be sure your students are on track. And, if they aren't, you have the necessary information to do something about it.

Identify the Golden Nuggets

09 Nearly every lesson we teach contains some golden nuggets. These are the key pieces of information students need to know. Or the key skills they need to be able to use if they want to be successful.

Identifying the golden nuggets for your lessons means you can make sure pupils understand these or get sufficient chance to practise them (if they are key skills).

For example, in a lesson introducing Macbeth, the golden nuggets might be:

- The relevance of the witches.

- Macbeth's relationship with his wife.

- The importance of passion and desire to the lead character's motivations.

Minimise Teacher Talk

10 Teacher talk can be important. In every lesson there needs to be some – even if it is just the teacher explaining what pupils need to do. But too much is often detrimental to learning.

Lecturing is not a hugely effective means by which to teach. It treats the mind like a bucket which ought to be filled, rather than as a garden which should be tended, cultivated and grown.

It encourages passivity which, in turn, encourages dependence.

Minimising teacher talk is therefore a means by which to encourage active thinking and independence; these are two habits central to success in nearly all walks of life.

Circulate

11 Circulating means moving around the room. If you are moving around the room then you are in a position to check the learning of all your students. In turn, this means you can talk to pupils, offer advice, ensure they remain on-task, ask questions and stretch their thinking.

By walking around the room while students are engaged in a task, you will be giving yourself the best chance to support everyone in your class.

For example, it might be that while circulating you observe an error in a student's work or hear a misconception surface during a discussion. In both cases you will be able to address the point at issue and help your pupils to progress beyond their current understanding. Such things are much harder to achieve if one does not circulate.

Ultimately, circulating is all about putting yourself in the best position to elicit information from your students (which you can then use to adapt your teaching and meet their needs).

Talk One-On-One

12 One-on-one conversations give you a chance to provide specific, targeted feedback to your students. This will put them in the best possible position to make great progress. Here are three ways you can build one-on-one conversations into your lessons:

- While pupils are engaged in a task, walk around the room and talk to individual students about their work.

- Set the class off on an extended activity (for example, a piece of independent writing). While this is happening, invite students up to the front to have one-on-one conversations with you focussing on where they are at and what they need to do to improve.

- Talk to pupils one-on-one about the most recent piece of work they have produced. Focus on the things they have done well and on one thing they need to do to improve.

Track

13 Outstanding teaching is not just about what you do in the classroom while your students are there. It is also concerned with what you do at other times as well. We touched on this in the first entry when we looked at planning. Here, we are thinking about tracking.

Tracking means keeping a close eye on how your pupils are performing over time. It means tracking their grades, their behaviour, their effort and their progress.

You can track all these things using a physical or an electronic markbook. Today, many schools buy database software such as Sims which you can also use for tracking purposes.

The great advantage of tracking is that it helps you to develop a sense of where pupils are going over time. You can identify trends, spot patterns and then respond to these in whatever way you feel is most appropriate.

Clarity, Clarity, Clarity

14 We mentioned earlier that teaching is fundamentally about communication. This means the clearer you communicate the better; clarity is a virtue in the classroom (as it is in most places).

If you are clear, your students will more quickly understand what it is you are trying to convey. This will speed up the learning process and minimise ambiguity.

Here are five areas where a focus on clarity can bring positive benefits:

- The language you use when explaining ideas.

- The language you use when giving instructions.

- The language you use when talking to students.

- The PowerPoint or IWB slides you use.

- Any resources you make for your pupils.

Are you ambiguous?

15 Staying with the themes of clarity and communication, it is worth asking yourself if you are ever ambiguous in the classroom.

If you are, what is this doing to your pupils?

It is providing them with mixed messages, a lack of intelligibility, and making it more likely that they will not do what it is you want them to do.

All of this stems from a lack of clarity.

By paying attention to the language you use and the way in which you communicate you will be in a better position to avoid ambiguity. In turn, this will make life easier for your pupils, leading to greater progress and more learning.

Use Your Body

16 Your body is a powerful tool. You can use it to great effect while teaching. Here are three examples of how:

- When talking to your class, use gestures to supplement your speech. These will help pupils to decode what you are saying. Body language is a key part of communication. By being aware of it you will be in a position to use it more effectively.

- Walk around the room. Just by doing this you will indicate to any students who are off-task that they should return to their work. Your presence will often be enough to channel them back along the right path.

- Keep your body language open and confident. This will help you to build rapport with your class. It will also send out positive messages about the fact that you are in control, organised and here to lead the learning.

Use Your Voice

17 Your voice is another important tool you have at your disposal. Used well it can have a significant impact on the effectiveness of your teaching. Here are three ideas you might like to try:

- Vary the tempo, pitch and pace of your voice. This will serve to increase the engagement and interest levels of your audience.

- Speak confidently and strongly but avoid shouting or becoming shrill. These latter two tend to put listeners off, invoking defence mechanisms (both physical and psychological).

- Inject some drama into your voice. If you are not sure how to do this, listen to a trained actor speaking in an interview or listen to a radio play, news report or the voice-over from a documentary. A dramatic delivery engages and interests the audience.

Use the Space

18 You can also use the space in your classroom as a means through which to teach well.

How you occupy space can have significant effects on others. For example, consider the difference between sitting in a corner of your room and standing at the front. Or, imagine the different response you might engender if, instead of remaining behind a desk, you strode around the room while giving instructions to your class.

You might also like to think about how you ask students to use the space in your room.

Perhaps you could alter the dynamic of your class by altering the seating arrangement. Alternatively, you could send out a message of equality and cooperation by asking pupils to sit in a circle.

Find Things to Praise

19 Pupils making great progress is a central feature of outstanding teaching. One of the keys to making progress in any area of life is motivation. If we are motivated, we are more likely to succeed. It's as simple as that.

Praise is a significant motivator. It makes us feel good about ourselves, builds positive connotations and provides us with information about what others deem to be good.

Finding things to praise students for is therefore an important means by which to build up motivation and, as a result, facilitate great progress.

It is particularly worthwhile looking for things to praise done by pupils who do not generally attract your attention. This way, you can try to ensure everyone in your class receives praise from you on a regular basis.

But Focus On Effort and Process

20 When giving out praise, focus on effort and process. It is clear what effort means and by process we mean the processes of thinking, doing and learning – as opposed to the end products which students produce.

The reason why this type of praise is more effective is as follows:

End products represent a culmination. They are the final, closed result of students' work. Effort is a habit; it is something we do, something we put in. Processes are also connected to habit. Our use and engagement with them can be cultivated over time.

As such, praising effort and process will help to habituate pupils into putting in effort and working hard at the processes which culminate in the production of their work.

Conversely, praising products will create psychological attachment to products and a failure to recognise that it is the prior work and learning which causes the product to exist.

For more on this point, see the work of the psychologist Carol Dweck, particularly her book *Mindset*.

Make failure great!

21 This may seem counter-intuitive, but stay with me.

Failure is how we learn.

When we fail at something, we gain a great deal of information. This concerns the reasons why we failed, how we went wrong, what didn't work and so forth. The flipside of this is that, when we succeed, we often don't receive much information explaining why things turned out well.

Failure nearly always gives us an insight. Success rarely does.

If you can help your students to appreciate this fact – if you can make them see that failure can be a great thing – then they will be in a much better position to take risks with their learning, try out new ideas and seek out challenges.

So celebrate failure. Reconceptualise it as a learning opportunity and encourage your pupils to take advantage of it wherever possible.

And Try to Use Misconceptions

22 Staying on the theme of getting things wrong, remember that student misconceptions are brilliant opportunities to make teaching points.

We want pupils to voice their misconceptions in class so that we can respond to them. If students don't share these then it is likely they will go on believing something which is incorrect.

You can encourage the verbalisation of misconceptions through providing opportunities for discussion, through questioning, through the use of questions specifically designed to draw out misconceptions, and through the use of open-ended questions which require students to explain and justify their answers.

When you spot a misconception, talk to pupils about it. Ask them to outline why they think like this. Then, go on to help them alter their thinking. If possible, use the misconception as an opportunity to talk to the whole class about whatever is at issue – the chances are that other pupils will have similarly faulty reasoning.

Use Great Activities

23 Great activities inspire, motivate and engage. They bring life and excitement to the lesson. They challenge students, stretching their thinking and encouraging them to look at ideas and information in active and, sometimes, innovative ways.

Outstanding teaching invariably includes great activities. Perhaps not all the time – after all, the constraints of the job mean this is simply not possible – but often enough that it has a significant impact of student achievement.

For a range of great activities see my book '50 Quick and Brilliant Lesson Activities,' available on Amazon.

Inject Some Fun

24 Fun creates engagement and builds positive connotations. Both of these will bind your students to your lessons, motivating them and helping them to make good progress.

It is not always possible to make lessons fun. Perhaps we would not want every lesson to be fun anyway; sometimes it is necessary to be quiet and focussed.

At the same time, injecting fun on a regular basis can have a good effect on your pupils. You can inject fun by using exciting activities, through humour, through variety, through challenges or games, through the use of drama (either in terms of activities or you adding drama to the learning) and, also, through engaging and inspirational questions or lesson aims.

Run a Tight Ship

25 Outstanding teaching nearly always involves the teacher and all their students pulling together. Running a tight ship is one important way to make sure this happens.

Not letting standards slip, picking up on small things, consistently modelling and conveying high expectations: all of these contribute to the maintenance of a tight ship. The emphasis has to be on the overall aim: outstanding teaching (and, as a result, outstanding learning).

To reinforce the point, consider the opposite. If we let small things slide, if we become loose in our approach and in our expectations, we are sending out the message that less than the best is good enough. And this is not want we want to convey if we are aiming for outstanding teaching!

Mix It Up

26 Variety has many benefits in the classroom:

- It creates engagement and motivation. This is a function of novelty and change within a context of repetition (the framework of the school day and the timetable).

- It offers students different ways in which to access and think about the learning.

- It plays to the different strengths pupils in your class might possess.

- It makes lessons and learning more memorable by differentiating them from one another.

- It gives you a chance to elicit information about your students' learning in different ways (which may reveal different things).

Overall, it is well worth mixing things up – both in terms of the lessons you plan and the way in which you teach them.

Give Great Feedback

27 Great feedback is the cornerstone of great learning. It facilitates progress by letting pupils know exactly what they need to do to improve.

Feedback can be verbal, written or non-verbal.

Verbal feedback involves you telling students something about their learning. This could be something they have done well or it could be something they need to do to improve.

Written feedback does the same thing but carries with it the advantage of being fixed across time and space. Therefore, students can refer to it again and again (or until they have successfully used the feedback!).

Non-verbal feedback includes things such as facial expressions, body language and gestures. It is not as powerful as the two other types of feedback but, equally, should not be overlooked completely.

Set Clear Targets

28 Leading on from great feedback is the idea of setting clear targets. A target is something you want students to do; a way in which they can improve the quality of their work. In short, a means by which they can make progress.

Clear targets are important because, if we want pupils to act on what we suggest, we need to be sure they can understand what we are asking. Hence, vagueness and ambiguity are the enemies here.

A clear target will give pupils enough information so that they know what they need to do, but not so much as to be overwhelming. It will be precise and specific, connected to the learning and suitable for implementation in the student's next piece of work.

Here is an example:

- Ensure you finish your essay with a conclusion. This should summarise the main points you have made and include your opinion on which way believe the evidence points.

Give Time to Targets

29 Having set clear targets for your pupils, it is important you give time to them during lessons. Otherwise, the targets cannot be successfully implemented. In fact, the most likely outcome is that students will forget, mislay or ignore them.

Here are three simple ways in which to give lesson time to targets:

- Include an activity closely related to the piece of work for which you gave targets. Ask students to put their targets into practice while completing this activity.

- Ask pupils to write their target immediately after the lesson title and then to try to put this into action through the course of the lesson.

- As the first activity, ask students to rewrite the piece of work you have marked, putting their target into action as they do.

Do Not Fear Repetition

30 A little earlier I suggested that variety brings many benefits (see entry 26). This is true. At the same time, one shouldn't fear repetition. And nor should one assume that repetition cannot be a part of outstanding teaching.

As a matter of fact, the reverse is true. Repetition is an important part of outstanding teaching.

We need to have students repeat things. This helps them to get better at those things. For example, writing essays week after week will generally lead to an improvement in the quality of the essay writing (particularly if great feedback and clear targets are given).

Make sure you include repetition in your teaching. Remember: practice makes perfect.

Do Not Fear Silence

31 A silent classroom concerns some teachers. They feel that a lack of noise is a bad thing; that an absence of voices signals an absence of learning.

This is not true.

At times we all need silence, not least as a basis for focussed, independent work.

So do not fear silence. Do not think that outstanding teaching happens only when pupils are talking.

Building periods of silence into your lessons is important. It provides an atmosphere in which pupils can pay full attention to that which is before them – the work they need to do. It also acts as preparation for exams and the kind of study you need to do in sixth form and at university if you are to be successful.

Do Not Fear Noise

32 Similarly, do not fear noise. Some teachers feel that noise is detrimental to learning, that it disrupts and damages the teaching environment. This general belief is not true.

What is true is that uncontrolled noise, noise which has no purpose, which does not connect to the learning, usually is detrimental. But noise which is the result of focussed, engaging activities is a good thing.

Students talking and discussing ideas and information are fundamental parts of good teaching. At times this might result in high levels of noise.

The key here is to retain a sense of control. By continuing to observe your class while they are being noisy, you will be able to ascertain in real-time whether or not the noise is contributing to the learning (and you will be able to spot if things tip over into the less effective side of things).

Set Your Boundaries and Then Police Them

33 Boundaries determine the extent of what you will allow in your classroom. They define acceptable behaviour and communicate your expectations to students. It may be that your boundaries alter over time as you grow more familiar with a class. It may be that they remain fixed throughout the year.

Whatever the case, it is important that you establish your boundaries early on (ideally, in the first lesson) and then police these rigorously.

Failure to do this will create inconsistency, ambiguity and uncertainty.

In the first instance, you will not be able to maintain consistency because you have no reference point. In the second, your students will not be clear as to what you expect. In the third, these first two factors will combine to create uncertainty, damaging your relationship with your class and making life harder for them than it needs to be.

Take Risks

34 It might seem strange at first glance to see risk-taking in a book on outstanding teaching. After all, you might reasonably assume that outstanding teaching involves consistency, familiarity and the use of tried and tested techniques (and this book is presenting you with a whole range of those).

However, effective risk-taking is something we find in many top-level performers (and this is definitely how we can classify outstanding teachers like yourself).

The reason is simple. As you reach the top of your game, you find yourself in a position of mastery. This, in turn, allows you to be creative. Risk-taking is about experimenting. Effective risk-taking is about experimenting from a position of mastery wherein one has sufficient knowledge and understanding to make reasonable predictions about what might happen.

Try Things Out

35 Continuing on the theme of risk and innovation consider the importance of trying things out in the context of outstanding teaching. If we want to maintain an outstanding level over time then we surely need to try new things. Otherwise, we risk becoming staid and rigid in our approach; we may very easily find ourselves descending into the ruts of familiarity, which can bring with them a sense of marking time.

You don't have to try big things out every time. It could just as easily be little things – a new starter activity; an adapted seating plan; or a question type you haven't used for a while.

When we try new things out we find ourselves in a position to collect information about their impact. We can use this information to refine our teaching. Hence, trying things out is as much about continuous improvement as it is about sustaining variety.

Reflect

36 When we reflect we look back at what we have done and ask ourselves questions.

- Did it work?

- What happened?

- How would I do things differently next time?

Reflection is a vital part of great teaching.

You can reflect during lessons, at break-time, at lunch-time or on your way home. Don't overdo it as this will lead to a waning of its effectiveness. But do make sure you do it regularly, in short bursts. Insights and new ideas will flow.

Survey Your Students

37 Surveying your students can bring all sorts of interesting results. You can use the information you elicit to inform your teaching. You may well find things out which would otherwise have remained beneath the surface.

Here are three simple ways to survey the pupils you teach:

- Produce a questionnaire and hand this out at the end of a term or unit of work. You can then collate the results.

- Use Survey Monkey, an online survey program, to create an electronic survey for your students to complete.

- If you have a managed learning environment, such as Frog or Fronter, create a forum and ask students to contribute their thoughts on your lessons.

Start With Success

38 Success feels good. It gives us confidence, lets us know we can achieve things.

All of this is motivational. Consider your own experiences. Chances are you have been more inclined to persist with activities where you experienced a degree of success early on.

By ensuring students experience success at the beginning of a lesson you can help bind them into that lesson. This creates a positive atmosphere, helping pupils to feel confident about their learning.

Confidence breeds success.

You do not need to make the start of your lessons incredibly easy (doing so is actually likely to have a negative effect in the long-term). Simply use starter activities which students can jump into straight away. You might base these on prior knowledge, past experience, opinions (which have to be justified) or recall of learning from the previous lesson.

However you choose to do it, helping pupils to start lessons successfully will bring big benefits.

End With Humour

39 Ending a lesson with humour, or even just a positive atmosphere engendered by some nice comments or a thank you, will see students leaving your room feeling good.

This will be the last thing they take away from the lesson. Chances are they will remember it (we tend to remember starts and ends more clearly than middles).

Upon returning to your classroom it is therefore likely they will arrive with a positive mindset.

Get Organised

40 Organisation is central to outstanding teaching. You need to know what you are doing, when you are doing it and why you are doing it.

You need to keep on top of your marking so that you can give timely, high-quality feedback.

You need to have all your resources ready well in advance of the lesson so as to ensure things run smoothly (and to provide yourself with the flexibility to respond if things don't go as you intend).

You need to be planned and ready to go well before the students arrive.

This is basic stuff but, all the same, many teachers fall down on some part of it. This seriously inhibits their chances of teaching consistently outstanding lessons.

Train Your Students

41 Training students means familiarising them with processes which form part of your teaching. These include:

- Routines at the start and end of lessons.

- Procedures for activities.

- Routines for self-assessment and the checking of one's work.

In each case, spending a little time training pupils will quickly reap rewards.

Training your students means they come to understand precisely what you expect of them in given situations. This will result in a lot of time being saved and a higher standard of work from the class as a whole (who know what they need to do, why they need to do it, and how it ought to be done).

Facilitate

42 The facilitator stands back. They provide a structure in which students can learn and then let them be independent. They watch and wait, stepping in when help or support is needed; sometimes offering a more challenging question to stretch a student's thinking.

Facilitation involves setting up activities which pupils can fully engage with and then letting them get on with things. It sees you ceding a degree of control; allowing the focus to move from you to the learning itself.

It is not always possible to facilitate.

Frequently, however, it is. And it is well worth taking advantage of such opportunities. This allows you to ensure all pupils actively engage with the learning and also lets you use your time more effectively (because you can observe who most needs your input and then give it to them).

Think Carefully Before Giving Out Grades

43 I say this because a large amount of research (see Black et al 2003) suggests that giving out grades has far less impact on achievement than giving out targets. And when the two are given together, the former detracts from the efficacy of the latter.

Of course, you should **always** record grades yourself in your markbook.

But you should think very carefully about when it is best to share these with students.

In an outstanding classroom, everybody's focus will be on learning. Targets are about learning. Targets facilitate progress. Grades are a function of the work we do and the progress we make. Therefore they do not add anything to learning in and of themselves.

My personal preference is to give regular targets, record all grades in my markbook, and share grades with students at pre-determined points in the year, making sure to keep these independent of targets so as not to decrease the latter's impact.

Make It Personal

44 Throughout this book we have been intimating that outstanding teaching involves making learning personal. This could be through feedback, through the activities you use, through your questioning, your interactions with students or the structure of your lessons.

Personalisation, or differentiation, means teaching which closely matches the needs of students.

Such teaching will almost always lead to better progress than the opposite.

For a wide range of activities, strategies and techniques through which to personalise learning, see my bestselling book 'How to use Differentiation in the Classroom: The Complete Guide.'

Ask Exciting Questions

45 Exciting questions cause students to think deeper and more interesting thoughts than boring questions. They engage, excite and motivate. They make us want to know what the answer might be.

You can use exciting questions:

- As lesson titles

- To introduce new topics

- When talking to individual students or groups

- When giving feedback

- Within activities

You might even like to develop a list of exciting questions connected to your topic. You can then keep this to hand, ready to call on whenever you feel it might be useful to pose an exciting question.

Play to Your Strengths

46 Because your strengths are the best thing about your teaching. And, therefore, they are probably the thing which helps your students to make the most progress.

If you are good at something – be it questioning, explaining, motivating or whatever – make use of this fact.

Consider Your Weaknesses

47 Because it might be that you can easily fix them. And, if so, think of what a difference this could make to your teaching.

And if you can't easily fix them, at least you know this and can take it into account while planning and teaching.

Be the Leader

48 Because if you're not leading the class, the learning, and the lesson, who is?

(Being the leader can also include facilitating leadership opportunities for students; though you will still be in overall control, guiding the ship as it were.)

Challenge Yourself

49 When striving for outstanding teaching this can be a difficult thing to do. Challenge may feel threatening. It takes us out of our comfort zone, pushing us in unfamiliar and potentially uncomfortable directions.

We learn through challenge though. It is by being challenged that we find out how far we can go and just what we are capable of.

Challenge allows us to discover new things, make changes we might never have considered, and operate in ways that might previously have felt inaccessible.

So challenging yourself, despite bringing difficulties, is a worthwhile enterprise. One that is likely to help you continue to be outstanding over an extended period of time.

Think Literacy

50 We conclude our tour of 50 quick ways to outstanding teaching by turning our attention to that which underpins nearly everything else: literacy.

Reading, writing, speaking and listening are central to learning. They form the basis of most of our interactions and also represent a high proportion of what goes on in school.

By attending to literacy during your lessons – thinking about how you can help your students to read, write, speak and listen better – you will be consolidating all the other fantastic work you are doing in order to be outstanding. In a way then, literacy is both the last word on the subject and the first.

A Brief Request

If you have found this book useful I would be delighted if you could leave a review on Amazon to let others know.

If you have any thoughts or comments, or if you have an idea for a new book in the series you would like me to write, please don't hesitate to get in touch at mike@mikegershon.com.

Finally, don't forget that you can download all my teaching and learning resources for **FREE** at www.mikegershon.com.

Printed in Great Britain
by Amazon.co.uk, Ltd.,
Marston Gate.